Hoppy Pet Rabbit Guide

By Aaron Webster

Forward:

Wind and clouds swirled through the skies with only the treetops blocking their incredible force. Way below the ferocious winds, there was a faint shadow of something running under the moonlit sky. The something carried a dim lantern and ran with weak but determined footsteps. A hurricane was coming and the footsteps belonged to me, a thirteen year old boy at the time who was desperately trying to protect his beloved rabbits...

My real name is Aaron Webster however many around the World prefer to call me by my earned alias "The Rabbit Master". I first began my rabbit adventure at age 10 when I purchased three rabbits with the purpose of raising and breeding them for 4-H. It didn't take me very long to fully realize this newly found passion and as a matter of fact by the time I graduated from High School, I had already raised and sold hundreds of rabbits and built up one of the most known rabbitries in the state of Texas. Over the last several years I have made it my goal to teach others everything that I have learned over the years about raising and caring for rabbits. That is why I decided to write a book a couple years ago titled: Raising Rabbits 101 and start the website RabbitBreeders.us which is now World famous. Since I received so much positive feedback from first book I decided it was time to write a sequel that would focus more on the "Pet Rabbit" side of the industry vs. breeding and selling, which is how this book came about.

A photo taken of me at age 15, holding "Hope" the rabbit.

Introduction:

I decided to write The Hoppy Pet Rabbit Guide with the purpose of providing the newbie rabbit enthusiast with a complete guide to getting started with a pet rabbit, and a guide that would teach them all the basic rabbit care essentials, through my own personal experience and conducted research. This book is meant to be a book that targets all ages of pet rabbit enthusiasts. Regardless of whether you are age 8, 88 or anywhere in-between, provided that you are indeed interested in owning a pet rabbit, this book is definitely for you.

If you make the decision and commitment to read this book from cover to cover, I can almost guarantee that by the end of this book you will have acquired all the information that you need to get started with a pet rabbit and effectively care for it.

In this pet rabbit care guide I will be essentially covering everything that you need to know to jumpstart yourself into the Pet Rabbit Industry and make your rabbit adventure worthwhile. In addition to reading this book I suggest that you check out the various resources that I have compiled and recommend throughout this pet rabbit guide, as doing so will help you learn more about rabbits in general and will help insure that you get the right supplies for your rabbit.

Good Luck and I Hope you Enjoy this Book,

Sincerely,

Aaron Webster

Author of: Hoppy Pet Rabbit Guide | Raising Rabbits 101

P.S: I would love to hear your thoughts, comments or suggestions about this book. Feel free to email me feedback at any time. My feedback email is <u>info@raisingrabbits101.com</u>. Also if you would like to potentially get a picture of yourself and beloved bunny included in the next edition of this book, feel free to send me pictures. Doing so will additionally give you a chance to win cool prizes :) THANKS!

Table of Contents

Contents

Chapter 1: Beginning Your Pet Rabbit Adventure

Interesting Facts about Rabbits

Rabbits are an incredibly interesting species that come in all different shapes, colors, breeds and sizes. Here is a listing of 15 interesting facts about rabbits:

1. Globally there are around 180 recognized breeds of rabbits. The leading organization, ARBA (American Rabbit Breeders Association) currently recognizes 47 breeds.

2. The record for the longest rabbit ears measured was 31.125 inches long.

3. Female rabbits are commonly referred to as "does" and male rabbits are likewise referred to as "bucks".'

4. The World record for a rabbit long jump is currently 3 meters.

5. Baby bunnies are commonly referred to as "kits" and bunnies from the same mother born at the same time are referred to as a "litter".

6. The record for the largest bunny rabbit litter ever reported was 24.

7. The teeth on a rabbit never stop growing.

8. Rabbits are not "rodents" rather their scientific classification is "lagomorphs".

9. The only place rabbits actually sweat is on the pads of their feet.

10. On average pet rabbits live longer than wild rabbits. Also rabbits that are raised indoors that don't have litters of bunnies, will usually live longer than those raised outdoors in rabbitries.

11. Rabbits actually have five toenails in their front paws and four toenails in their back paws.

12. Several of the wild species of rabbits found in North America include; cottontails, jackrabbits and snowshoe rabbits.

13. At the time of this writing, the World's heaviest rabbit is named Darius, weighing an unprecedented 50 pounds.

14. Bunnies are actually born furless with their eyes closed.

15. Throughout history rabbits have been commonly used in religion and mythical symbolism. For instance, the Aztecs believed in a pantheon of 400 rabbit gods which represented fertility, parties and drunkenness.

Reasons to Own a Pet Rabbit

In theory I believe that if everyone knew even half of what I know about rabbits, for every person who owns a cat, there would be at least one person who would potentially choose to own a rabbit. <u>Here is a list of reasons why I believe rabbits make such great pets:</u>

1. **Rabbits literally come in all different shapes and sizes** – I have found from personal observation that very few people realize the huge variety of rabbit breeds available. Most people just assume rabbits are all very similar in size and appearance. The fact of the matter is that, this couldn't be further from the truth. Just like it has been said that "there is a breed of dog to fit each individual". I honestly believe that "there is a breed of rabbit to fit each individual". Want a small rabbit that you can hold in your palms full grown? No problem, get a Britannia Petite. Want a huge rabbit that will make your friends and family literally fall over in astonishment? No problem, get a Flemish Giant. Want a rabbit with adorably long ears and a tame personality? Get a breed of Lop. Want a breed of rabbit with long fur that resembles wool? No problem, there are Angora Rabbits waiting in cages at rabbitries at this very moment, waiting for you to come take them home.

2. **Rabbits are naturally tame animals** – I have found that naturally most rabbits are tame animals. As long as you let them get used to you at a fairly early age and select a more pet oriented breed, they will almost always allow you to pet and cuddle them.

3. **Rabbits are very quiet animals** – At the very moment I am writing this message my dog is standing outside my room door barking once again, for no real apparent reason. You can rest assured that rabbits won't ever cause you or your neighbors this sort of agitation as they are naturally extremely quiet animals. In fact the only time rabbits will make noise is when they are hurt or terrified by something, if they are you will usually hear them squeal to alert you.

4. **Rabbits are fairly easy to train** – When owning a rabbit, especially one of the pet breeds I recommend in this book, you can rest assured that if you wish you can train them pretty easily to do things such as use a litter box.

5. **Rabbits are Low Maintenance Animals** – Although it is recommended that you spend some time with your rabbit each and every day. Compared to most dogs and even many cats, rabbits are low maintenance animals.

6. **Rabbits naturally are clean animals** – Similar to cats, rabbits will generally stay pretty clean as they lick themselves down frequently. Also I have noticed that if you keep multiple rabbits together, many times they will give each other "tongue baths".

7. **Rabbits are fairly low cost animals** – When buying a pet rabbit usually you will pay less than $100 regardless of the breed, compared to several times that price for a purebred dog.

8. **Rabbits are simply AWESOME and make nice pets** – Ok maybe I'm a bit biased since I'm "The Rabbit Master" however I truly believe rabbits are about the best type of pet you can own. They are AWESOME animals, enough said. :)

Responsibility of Owning a Pet Rabbit

While rabbits do indeed make great pets, you need to understand the amount of responsibility required in taking care of them (just like any other animal), before rushing out on impulse to go buy one. Too many rabbits are bought by unprepared owners on impulse and then dropped back off at already full shelters within a couple months.

<u>You need to be prepared to feed, water and care for your bunny rabbit each and every day.</u> If you are not prepared to spend at least a little time each day with your new rabbit, don't get one. **Pet rabbits shouldn't be treated like toys, that are left on a shelf (or cage in this case) and only taken out every once in awhile.** Instead they should be treated as companions and given frequent attention.

Also you need to understand that if you purchase one of the larger rabbit breeds as a bunny, they will indeed grow to be a "big bunny", within a couple months, and not just stay small forever.

 **If you want this little bunny for Easter**

 **but don't want this big bunny for 7-12 years**

 **then get this little bunny for Easter instead**

www.magichappensrescue.com

Cost of a Pet Rabbit

By Ellyn (RabbitSmarties.com)

Keeping a pet rabbit certainly isn't free. Beyond the original purchase price, there are many costs involved with keeping any pet. But relative to larger animals such as cats or dogs, it's extremely affordable to keep a pet rabbit.

Cost of Supplies for First Rabbit Purchase

You can buy a brand-new, high quality cage for your pet, plus feeding and watering equipment, for well under $100. Add all the toys, feed, and accessories you want, and your startup equipment costs should still be between $125-200 if you purchase from a supplier that offers competitive prices, like **PremiumRabbits.com**. Isn't it great that rabbits are so affordable compared to other pets!

How much is that bunny in the window?

Someone might give you a free pet rabbit, or you might pay as much as $100 for one. The cost of your pet will depend not so much on the rabbit's quality, but the place where you buy it. Pet stores usually ask over $50. If you buy straight from a pet or show rabbit breeder, you will probably pay $30-$50. A farmer or farm store may charge less. The difference in price probably won't be enough that it should be a determining factor as you decide where to buy your pet. It's much more important to choose a seller who has clean facilities and takes excellent care of each of their animals.

Additional Costs of Keeping a Pet Rabbit

Once you've got equipment, feed, bedding, and a bunny purchased, there aren't a lot of other expenses you will need to cover. The good news is that rabbits do not need regular vaccinations or check-ups at the veterinarian's office. Many rabbits live their whole lives without seeing a vet! However, you should always have a little cash set aside in case of an emergency situation where your bunny needs medical help.

Pet Rabbit Breed Selection

One of the most critical yet exciting parts of Getting Started in the Rabbit World is choosing your rabbit breed. You ideally want to choose a rabbit breed that is ideal for your specific purpose. Since you are seeking to own a pet rabbit you will want to select a breed that is naturally pretty tame and that you can effectively handle.

Although there are a huge number of different rabbit breeds that you can potentially choose from here are a listing of the ones I most recommend for pets...

My Top 4 Favorite Pet Rabbit Breeds:

- Holland Lops (My Favorite Choice – Very Nice Friendly Animals – Easy to find)
- Mini Lops (Definitely one of the cutest breeds)
- Mini Rex (Small and friendly – Come in many colors)
- Netherland Dwarfs (My Second Favorite – Tiny + Cute – Easy to find)

Holland Lops:

Holland Lop Rabbit Pictures:

Mini Lop Rabbit Pictures:

Mini Rex Rabbit Pictures:

Netherland Dwarf Rabbit Pictures:

Out of all the rabbit breeds in existence my top four personal recommendations for a newbie pet rabbit owner would be; Holland Lops, Mini Lops, Mini Rex and Netherland Dwarfs. These four breeds are all small in size, are generally nice and friendly animals, easy to care for and there are a plentiful supply of breeders. Regardless of where you live you should pretty easily be able to find breeders of these rabbits, especially the Holland Lops and Netherland Dwarfs (my personal favorites).

Some Other Great Pet Rabbit Breeds:

- Dutch (Small rabbits that are known for their black and white appearance)
- Dwarf Hotots (Very small breed – all white with dark circles around its eyes)
- English Angoras (Large and Fluffy)
- English Lops (Larger with very long ears)
- Flemish Giants (Very large friendly animals – Size is great for impressing a friend)
- Lionheads (Another nice pet rabbit breed however they are not yet ARBA recognized)
- Himalayans (Small and cute with a white body and black markings)

Note: While these are the rabbit breeds that I currently recommend the most for pets, if you fall in love with a different breed feel free to go with it. Different people have different rabbit preferences :)

Dutch Rabbit:

Dwarf Hotot Rabbit:

English Angora Rabbit:

English Lop Rabbit:

Flemish Giant Rabbit:

Lionhead Rabbit:

Himalayan Rabbit:

What is your favorite rabbit breed and why?

"Holland Lops. Every Holland has its own personality. Some are quiet and reserved while others are easily excited. Not to mention the cute factor with the lopped ears."

-Kimberly Kramer (Idaho)

"English Angoras, nothing compares to having a big, fluffy bunny to run your fingers through all that wool. It's like touching a cloud and getting bunny kisses."

-Phyllis Carroll (Florida)

"Mini Rex. They are so soft and so calm and friendly."

-Charity Sutherland (Alaska)

"The lionhead 2x ... because they are so soft and nice. They like to play and are very sociable. They are loving pets. I like all long fur breeds!"

-Lydia Pacheco (Quebec)

47 Breeds of Rabbits Photo Gallery

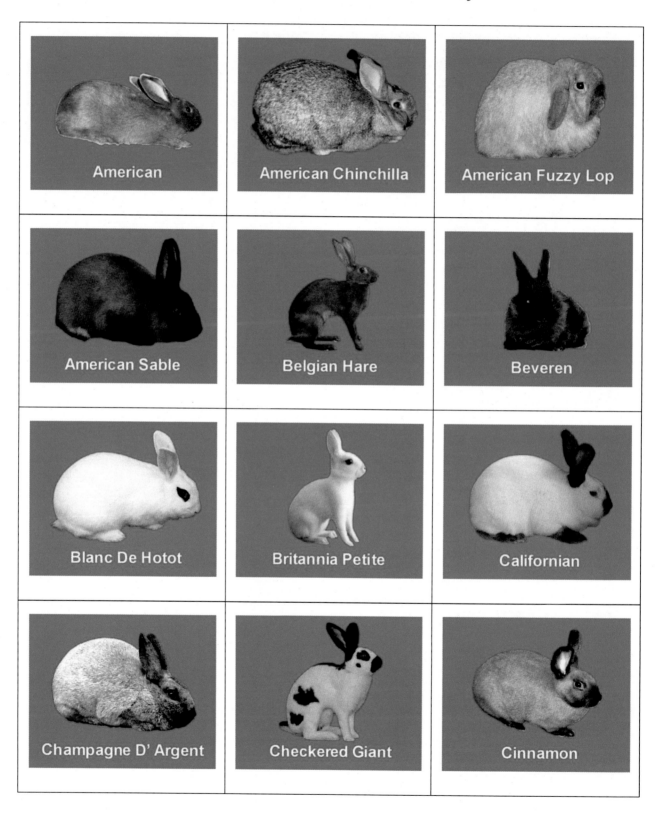

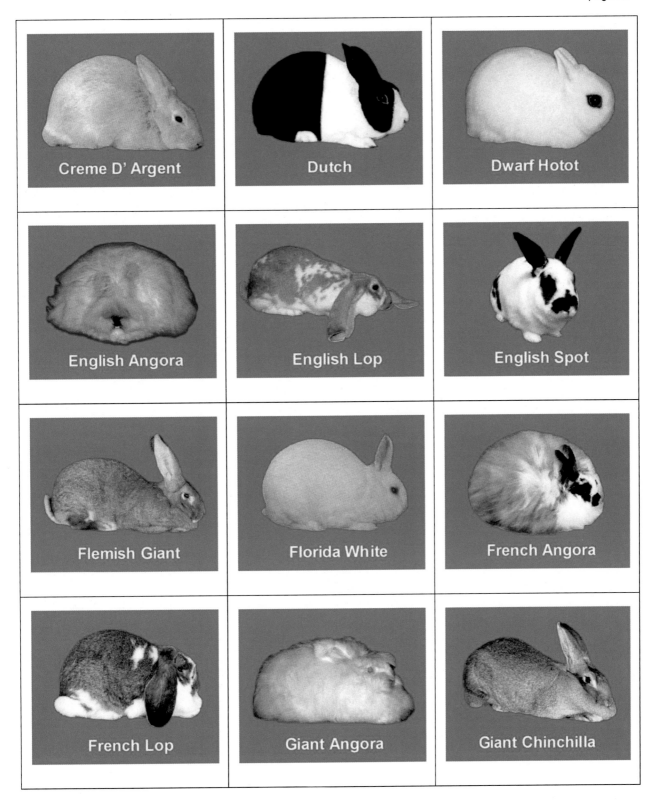

Creme D' Argent | Dutch | Dwarf Hotot

English Angora | English Lop | English Spot

Flemish Giant | Florida White | French Angora

French Lop | Giant Angora | Giant Chinchilla

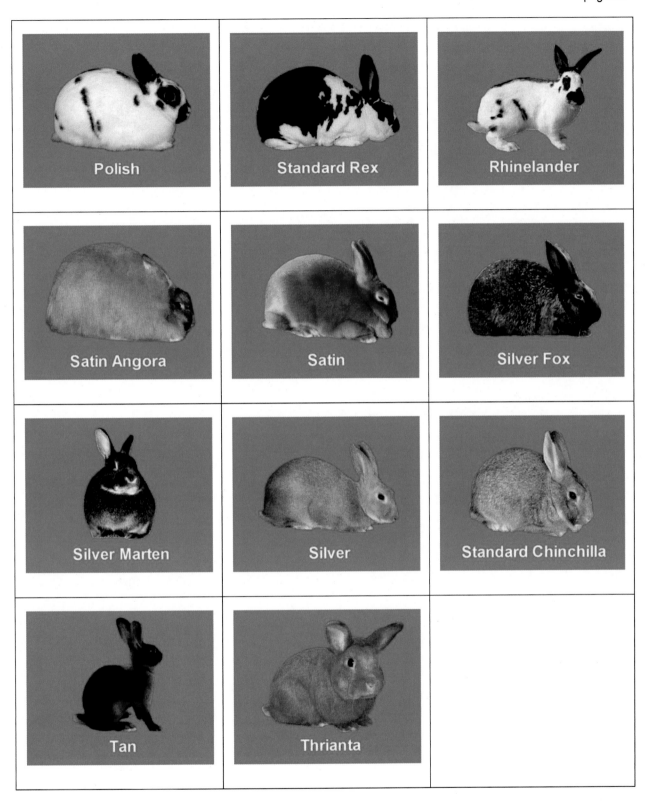

Breeds of Rabbits Average Size Chart

Breed	Weight	Size
American	10-11 lbs	Large
American Chinchilla	9-11 lbs	Large
American Fuzzy Lop	3.5-3.75 lbs	Small
American Sable	8-9 lbs	Medium
Belgian Hare	6-9.5 lbs	Medium
Beveren	8-11 lbs	Large
Blanc de Hotot	8-11 lbs	Large
Britannia Petite	2.5 lbs	Small
Californian	8-10 lbs	Large
Champagne D' Argent	9-11 lbs	Large
Checkered Giant	11.5 + lbs	Giant
Cinnamon	8-11 lbs	Large
Crème D' Argent	8-11 lbs	Large
Dutch	3-5 lbs	Small
Dwarf Hotot	2.5-3 lbs	Small
English Angora	6-9 lbs	Medium
English Lop	9-10 lbs	Large
English Spot	6-8 lbs	Medium
Flemish Giant	13 + lbs	Giant
Florida White	4-6 lbs	Small
French Angora	6-9 lbs	Medium
French Lop	10.5-11 lbs	Large
Giant Angora	9-11 lbs	Large
Giant Chinchilla	12-15 lbs	Giant
Harlequin	6.5-9 lbs	Medium
Havana	4.5-6 lbs	Small
Himalayan	3-5 lbs	Small
Holland Lop	3-4 lbs	Small
Jersey Wooly	3-3.5 lbs	Small
Lilac	5.5-7.5 lbs	Medium
Mini Lop	4.5-6 lbs	Small
Mini Rex	3-4.5 lbs	Small
Mini Satin	3-6 lbs	Small
Netherland Dwarf	2-2.5 lbs	Small
New Zealand	9-11 lbs	Large
Palomino	9-10 lbs	Large
Polish	2.5-3.5 lbs	Small
Rex	7-9 lbs	Medium
Rhinelander	6-9 lbs	Medium

Satin	9-11 lbs	Large
Satin Angora	6-9 lbs	Medium
Silver	4-6 lbs	Small
Silver Fox	9-11 lbs	Large
Silver Marten	6-9 lbs	Medium
Standard Chinchilla	5-7 lbs	Medium
Tan	4-6 lbs	Small
Thrianta	7-9 lbs	Medium

Don't believe the gigantic rabbit in the photo above is real?

Check out the Washington Times Article here for proof:

http://tinyurl.com/ys8335

Buying vs Adopting Debate

One of the topics that commonly come up when someone is deciding to get a rabbit, is whether or not they should adopt. So in this article I am going to give you my recommendation and address the pros and cons of adopting.

Adopting a Rabbit Pros and Cons:

The biggest Pro to adopting a rabbit is the fact that you will many times be giving an abandoned rabbit a home it might not otherwise have. That being said, when you buy a pet rabbit from a breeder, technically you are doing the same thing. If nobody was to come and purchase that rabbit, it would probably just go on sitting there in a cage at the breeder's home.

The biggest Con to adopting a rabbit is that doing so will generally limit your selection and you may end up with a rabbit that isn't as easy to care for or train. Also making the decision to spay or neuter usually isn't optional in this case, meaning that you will most likely never be able to breed that rabbit in the future.

One misconception about "Adopting" is that it is free; usually however this is not the case. Most rescue centers and other places of that nature will charge you an adoption fee and may make you additionally pay to have your rabbit spayed or neutered.

The Advantage of Buying: The main advantage of buying your rabbit is the fact that you will be able to choose the exact rabbit breed that you would like to own and usually have a greater selection of animals to choose from. You will also be able to make the decision on your own regarding whether or not to spay/neuter your bunny.

Should I Buy or Adopt... My Advice: My advice is that if you are just starting out in the rabbit World you should first choose a rabbit breed that you like and then buy from a breeder. Later on if you decide to get another rabbit, then you can consider adopting rather than right away when you don't have any hands on experience. Several pet rabbit owners who have adopted bunnies from rescue shelters have informed me that those bunnies tend to need more care as they may have suffered from previous trauma in their life (not always ideal for the newbie).

Buying your Rabbit

If you would like to own a pet rabbit my advice is that you seek to purchase your rabbit from a dedicated rabbit breeder who has experience in the industry.

I wouldn't necessarily recommend getting a pet rabbit from just anyone; instead you should aim to buy from a reputable individual who takes good care of their rabbits.

You can find many reputable rabbit breeders on a rabbit breeder's directory website that I assembled over the last several years together titled: RabbitBreeders.us. On the website you can literally find a listing of over 1,800 rabbitries from across the country. These breeders range from the small hobby breeder with around 10 rabbits to the large commercial rabbitry with 100s or even 1000s of rabbits.

Check it out: http://rabbitbreeders.us/

Utilizing this special rabbit breeder's directory website that I created you can search for rabbit breeders in your area by breed and state. To find a breeder all you have to do is browse through the different breeder listings, find one in your area and then utilize their provided contact information to get in touch.

Note: Some breeds are harder to find than others: If you are looking to find a Holland Lop Rabbit Breeder in your area, it most likely won't be too hard; however some of the rarer breeds naturally don't have a ton of listings within our directory.

Quick Tip: If you can't find a breeder of a specific breed on the breed page, I still suggest that you browse your state page as we only list a breeder's specified main breed within the breed pages of our directory.

In addition to setting up RabbitBreeders.us I have also established two sister directory websites; one for England and one for Canada. The website urls of those websites are RabbitBreeders.org.uk for England and RabbitBreeders.ca for Canada.

Rabbit Breeder Directories

Please check out the Rabbit Breeder Directory websites listed below (created by myself) to find rabbits for sale in your area and state (province or territory in you live outside the USA), or search for rabbits for sale by breed.

United States: http://rabbitbreeders.us/

Canada: http://www.rabbitbreeders.ca/

England: http://rabbitbreeders.org.uk/

How to Tell if a Rabbit is a Boy or a Girl

If you own a rabbit or are thinking about getting one, it is a good idea for you to learn how to determine whether any rabbit put in front of you, is a boy or a girl. Here is a step by step tutorial on how to do so.

Step 1: First locate the rabbit that you would like to sex and move it to a flat surface.

Step 2: Next take a hold of the rabbit's tail with one hand and lift it upwards a little bit, or if you feel comfortable enough handling your rabbit you can cradle it in your arms while trying to determine its sex.

Step 3: Use two fingers to press down on your rabbit's vent area which is just in front of the anus. If the rabbit is a male his part should protrude. If the rabbit is a female you should see a slit or central line running up and down.

Quick Tip: If you are having trouble figuring out how to sex a rabbit by yourself, find another rabbit owner in your area who can teach you hands on.

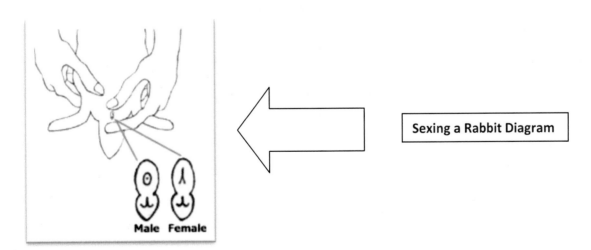

Sexing a Rabbit Diagram

When a rabbit is older the sex becomes obvious: Once a rabbit is several months old its sex becomes more obvious. Females will develop dewlaps on their chins and the reproductive sacks on the males will become visible if you flip them over. Personally I can just look at a rabbit now and usually tell its sex by the shape of its head and overall appearance.

Pet Rabbit Supplies

By Ellyn (RabbitSmarties.com)

Are you planning on getting a pet rabbit? Congratulations! You made a wonderful choice, because pet rabbits not only make excellent companions, but they are easy to care for. All you need is a little time to care for it, a little space for it to live, and the right equipment.

Required Supplies for keeping Pet Rabbits

One of the most important things you can provide for your rabbit is suitable housing. Even if you plan to let your bunny roam around your home, he MUST have a cage he can call his own and return to if he ever gets frightened.

Home Sweet Hole

The cage doesn't need to be huge. In fact, many bunnies are more comfortable with a small, close "hole" to live in. Ideally, the cage should have galvanized wire sides and flooring. Wire floors might not sound nice at first, but actually researchers showed that rabbits preferred wire floors when given an option! Wire floors are much easier to clean and allow your rabbits to stay healthy, because they aren't sitting in their urine. You will want a wire-floored cage with a slide-out drop tray, like the Supreme Rabbit Homes" at **PremiumRabbits.com**. Their "small" size is a 18x24" cage is a great size for any dwarf breed, such as a Holland Lop or Polish.   They also have larger sizes of Supreme Rabbit Homes for larger breeds.

Bunnies need Kitchenware, too!

Bunnies definitely enjoy eating, so it's important to provide them with feeding and watering equipment that is safe and comfortable to use. When you are buying a food dish, the number one question to ask is "can my rabbit tip this over?" If a rabbit can spill his food all over the floor, he almost certainly will, so it's important to buy a dish that hooks on to the cage wire (check out the EZ-crock from **PremiumRabbits.com**) or a heavy ceramic crock.

You can use a ceramic crock for water, also. However, many people opt to use water bottles instead, because they keep the water cleaner. A 16 ounce water bottle works great for most bunnies. Just check it every day to make sure it is full. If you take your rabbit on a trip with you, you may want to use an eight-ounce travel size bottle while are gone.

Other Supplies Recommended

If you have a cage with a drop tray, and feed and watering equipment, you are pretty good to go! You will probably need other supplies in the future, but those depend on what you plan to do with your rabbit. If you want to house train it, you will need a litter box with bedding. If you plan to breed it, you must obtain a nest box. If you want to teach it to jump hurdles, you will need a harness and some jumps. You can shop through many types of rabbit accessories at **PremiumRabbits.com**.

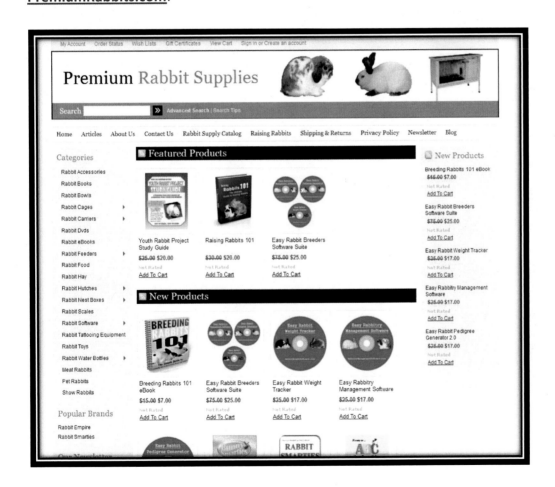

Shop for Rabbit Supplies for sale: http://PremiumRabbits.com/

Getting Started Overview

In Chapter #1 of this book I have discussed all the major topics associated with getting started with your pet rabbit project.

So far in this book I have already covered the topics of; Pet Rabbit Breed Selection, Cost of a Pet Rabbit, Reasons to Own a Pet Rabbit, Interesting Facts about Rabbits, How to Tell if a Rabbit is a Boy or a Girl, Pet Rabbit Supplies and Purchasing your Rabbit Supplies.

This means that if you have been following along closely, you should have just about all the information at your fingertips that you need to begin your pet rabbit adventure.

To start off Chapter #2 of this book I will be covering the topic of feeding your pet rabbit. So before you actually go out and buy your first rabbits you may want to go ahead and read that section of this book as well.

If you are looking for information about Pet Rabbit Interaction, check out Ch 3 of this book.

Chapter 2: Caring for Your Pet Rabbit

Feeding Your Pet Rabbit

By Ellyn (RabbitSmarties.com)

Finding the right diet for your pet rabbit is extremely important, right? In the wild, rabbits live on roughage and their digestive systems need a lot of fiber to function properly. At the same time, they need enough energy to grow and thrive. Finding a good balance between fiber, energy, and freshness in rabbit diets used to be very difficult for rabbit owners. Thankfully, now we can rely on pelleted feed to make sure our rabbits get complete nutrition.

But not all rabbit feed is created equal -- oh no! Not by a long shot. Peruse the rabbit feed section at your local pet store and you will see a huge variance in fiber content, protein content, ingredients, and pellet color. Ideally, adult and junior rabbits should have at least 20% fiber in their diets, and 15-18% protein. The pellets should be green and smell fresh.

The best pellet brand that this author has ever seen is Sherwood Forest Natural Rabbit Food. David Sherwood, a nutritionist and long-time rabbit breeder, developed a line of rabbit food that is not only carefully formulated for rabbits needs at different stages of life, but is made with only fresh and wholesome ingredients. When Mr. Sherwood introduced his new feed a few years ago, thousands of rabbit owners quickly switched to it and feed it exclusively. You can get more information, read rave reviews, or give it a try at **PremiumRabbits.com**.

Beyond the Pellets

Besides a high-quality pellet, rabbits need clean water. A rabbit will not eat unless it has plenty of fresh water to drink also. Besides pellets and water, hay is a very beneficial part of a rabbit's diet. In fact, one type of Sherwood Natural Rabbit Food is designed to be offered in half-pellets, half-hay ratio.   No matter what brand of pellets you feed, fresh Timothy hay will complement it.

But what about vegetables?

When you're meeting your rabbit's nutritional needs through a pelleted diet, there's little reason to offer fruits or vegetables and they can actually do your bunny harm. Any treats, be they grain, fruit, or veggie, can upset the balanced nutrition in the pellets if you give them in great qualities. However, everyone loves to give their bunnies a special snack now and then. In those cases, dandelion leaves, carrots, and apples make good treats. Avoid light green lettuce, as it tends to give rabbits a tummy ache.

Shop for Rabbit Food for sale: http://PremiumRabbits.com/

Pet Rabbit Health

When owning a pet rabbit it is important to monitor the health of your rabbit, and be able to make an educated guess whether or not your rabbit requires treatment of some sort.

Here is a listing of signs that may suggest that your rabbit is sick and requires treatment:

- Your rabbit stops eating its food (the surest sign that something is up).

- Your rabbit begins sneezing more than would seem natural.

- Your rabbit stops drinking water

- Your rabbit develops abscesses or lumps of some sort on its skin.

- Your rabbit begins to discharge white stuff out of its nose.

- Your rabbit starts losing patches of fur (with the exception to seasonal molting).

- Your rabbit begins to shake its ears a lot more than normal.

- Your rabbit starts acting unnaturally aggressive.

- Your rabbit simply begins to exhibit aberrant behavior.

If you are sure that your rabbit is sick you can do one of three things; 1. Try and treat the sickness/condition yourself. 2. Bring your rabbit to a vet. 3. Watch and Wait.

3 Sicknesses/Conditions that you can easily treat yourself:

- **Ear Mites** – This condition like the name suggests is caused by a mite infestation within the ear of your rabbit. If you notice that your rabbit has yellow crusty looking stuff in its ear, it may very well be "ear mites". Although "ear mites" can potentially be deadly if it isn't properly treated, to treat the condition all you have to do is apply some mineral oil into the rabbit's ear every few days until it goes away. If you notice your rabbit shaking its head quite a bit more than normal, I suggest that you check to make sure it doesn't have any mites as that can indeed be a sign of the condition.

- **Fur Mites** - If you notice that your rabbit is losing patches of fur in a way that skin is left bare, there is a good chance that your rabbit has fur mites. To treat fur mites many rabbit raisers have found that all that you have to do is give your rabbit a bath using some cat shampoo. Personally I haven't had many cases of fur mites in all my years of raising rabbits however it you have dogs and cats near your rabbits this condition tends to be more common.

- **Weepy Eyes** – If your rabbit has a section of matted fur in the corner of its eye or there is noticeable discharge in the eye area there is a good chance that your rabbit has a condition called Weepy Eyes. To treat this condition all you need to do is apply some ophthalmic ointment to the eye twice a day for several days or until the eye heals.

Note: In my book Raising Rabbits 101 available at discount via RaisingRabbits101.com I dedicate an entire chapter to treating rabbit sicknesses/illnesses, so if you are interested in learning more about how to treat the sickness/condition yourself I suggest that you grab yourself a copy of the book.

2. Bring your rabbit to a vet

If you notice that your rabbit is pretty sick and you don't know what to do about it, it is a good idea to take your rabbit to the vet. Making the decision to bring your rabbit to the vet can potentially save its life; however be warned vet visits can be costly.

If interested you can find a listing of vets that specialize in rabbits via:

http://rabbit.org/rabbit-veterinarians-state-listings/

3. Watch and Wait

Depending upon the severity of the sickness/condition that your rabbit has, you may just want to watch and wait for a little while before rushing off to take your rabbit to the vet. Many times rabbits can have sicknesses/conditions that will go away on their own provided the rabbit is getting adequate nutrition and care. In this case you will just have to rely on your own best judgment not mine.

Should I Spay or Neuter my Pet Rabbit?

A common question that newbie pet rabbit owners ask is; Should I Spay or Neuter my Pet Rabbit? In this article I will be addressing some of the pros and cons to making the decision to spay or neuter your rabbit.

PROS:

- Spaying/Neutering can prevent annoying behaviors when your rabbit reaches sexual maturity such as potentially; spraying urine, biting, an increase in chewing and digging, and other behaviors of that nature.

- Some studies have shown that by spaying/neutering your rabbit, its lifespan will usually increase by a substantial amount.

- Spayed/Neutered rabbits will generally have much reliable litter box habits than those who haven't undergone the procedure.

- Lastly when your rabbit is spayed/neutered you will never run the risk of accidently ending up with unwanted litters of bunnies. **Note**: Rabbits can indeed multiple like rabbits in many cases.

CONS:

- Spaying/Neutering will eliminate the ability for you to breed your rabbit in the future.

- Spaying/Neutering your pet rabbit can be fairly costly just like the procedure for dogs or cats. That being said, cost in my opinion should not be the determining factor in this case unless you plan on owning multiple pet rabbits.

Conclusion: Unless you plan on breeding your rabbit in the future I highly recommend that if you want to have an indoor pet (recommended) that you go ahead and get the rabbit spayed (procedure for females) or neutered (procedure for males).

Note: Usually rabbits are spayed/neutered between 3 and 6 months of age.

Chapter 3: Interacting with Your Pet Rabbit

Pet Rabbit Behaviors and Meanings

By Ellyn (RabbitSmarties.com)

Rabbits "speak" almost entirely with body language. Unlike cats, dogs, or guinea pigs, rabbits almost never make vocal noises. But by studying rabbit body language, you can learn how to get along well with your new pet. Here are just a few rabbit behaviors that you should be familiar with:

Stamping or Thumping

Thumper from Bambi is famous for beating his hind foot on the ground, and pet rabbits will do this, too. (The only difference is that real rabbits just stamp once at a time, instead of repeatedly.) Stamping or thumping is a sign that a rabbit is excited, alarmed, or very peeved with his owner. It's not necessarily a warning that danger is nearby. Thumping can be contagious: if you have multiple rabbits living in the same room, one thump may cause others to start thumping too.

Teeth Clicking

Rabbits will sometimes click or chatter their teeth when they are content. It's sort of the equivalent of a cat's purr. The sound is very soft and you will only notice it if your rabbit is relaxed and comfortable. You can actually see the jaw moving as rabbits click their teeth.

Teeth grinding is very different. Rabbits will only grind their teeth if they are in great pain. The sound is loud and unmistakable. If you hear your rabbit grind its teeth, take it to the vet right away.

Lunging or Biting

It's no fun to see your pet lunge at you with its mouth open, ready to tear your flesh. Thankfully most rabbits never do this. If your rabbit lunges at you unexpectedly, but is usually friendly, don't worry too much. He's probably just having a bad day. Give him his space until he's feeling better.

Unfortunately, a few rabbits are chronic biters. These just usually have the "mean gene" and there's not much you can do to correct it. It's very important to never breed a rabbit that has a bad attitude.

Binky

On a much more pleasant note comes the Binky or the Jump-Wiggle. This gesture happens when a rabbit is so happy he jumps for joy. If your rabbit is running around in its playpen and suddenly leaps sideways or straight up in the air, he's just enjoying his life. Rabbits often seem taken by surprise by their own jump-wiggles, as if it was something they do involuntarily.

Ear Movement

The position of your rabbit's ears can tell you a lot about how he is feeling. If his ears are laid back against his head, then he is relaxed and off his guard. If they are upright and cocked, he is listening to something. Be gentle around your bunny when he is listening, as a sudden noise or movement might frighten him. If his ears pitch forward suddenly, it can be a sign of aggression.

Training your Pet Rabbit

By Ellyn (RabbitSmarties.com)

The more time you spend with your new pet, the more you will enjoy him. As you get to know your rabbit you can train it, much in the way you can train a dog.

House Training

If you keep your bunny in your home and don't want to keep it shut up in its cage all day, you can train it to urinate in a litter box. This type of training is best begun when your rabbit is still young, such as eight to twelve weeks of age. Keep your rabbit in its cage until it selects one corner as its "potty spot." Then move the litter box into that corner of the cage. When your rabbit has gotten used to using the litter box, you can open his cage door and let him run around the floor of a closed room in your house. Watch him closely, and if he starts to urinate anywhere besides in his cage, stop him by saying "no!" and shooing him back to his cage. Once he has learned to urinate in his box, you can let him run around the rest of your home. Some rabbits will always leave dry droppings outside of the cage, but that is normal and not a big concern.

Chew Prevention

One problem with having a house rabbit is that he will probably chew on anything he can find. This is not only damaging to your furnishings, but could be harmful to your bunny if he chews on electrical wire or toxic paint. If you can, try to keep things out of the rabbit's reach, but you can also train him to stop chewing at the command "no!"

Clicker Training -- Teaching a Rabbit Tricks

Rabbits can be trained to do all kinds of tricks: jump hurdles, come when called, give kisses, and even walk on their hind legs. The most effective way to train a rabbit is with a "clicker." Find out what treat your bunny likes best and then teach him to associate that treat with the sound of a clicker. Then sit down with your rabbit in a small play pen. Play with him until he performs a behavior that you want to replicate, then click the clicker and give him a treat. (Always wait till the rabbit does the behavior naturally. For instance, if you want to teach him to walk on his hind legs, wait till he stands up on his hind legs of his own accord, and then click the clicker. Don't try to lift him on to his hind legs – he will probably wind up confused.) Clicker training is most effective before a bunny has had its full meal for the day, while he is active and interested in his surroundings.

In training, it's also very important to teach a rabbit its name. As soon as you get your bunny, pick a name for him and repeat it many times in his hearing. Say his name as you pet him in his favorite spot. Say his name when you give him a treat. Set him down on one side of a room, then walk to the other side, call his name and make eye contact with him. If you can teach your rabbit to respond to his name, you will have come a long way toward teaching him new tricks.

Chapter 4: Exclusive Bonus Section

Pet Rabbit Owner Interview #1

Name

Olivia Winsley

Location (City, State/Province, Country)

Chew stoke, England

About how long have you been a pet rabbit owner?

5 years

What made you want to own a rabbit?

I just wanted a rabbit because I thought that that were calm and loving pets to have.

What is your favorite pet rabbit breed and why?

Netherland dwarf because they are the smallest breed you can get and they are really cute! Tiny ears!

What advice would you give to a brand new pet rabbit owner?

I would say just handle, feed and water it daily. Also train it to use a litter tray so that you can simply clean that out.

Do you own more than one pet rabbit? Why or why not?

Yes I own 3 pet bunnies all of the same breed because I really wanted rabbits!

Is your pet rabbit spayed or neutered? Why or why not?

He is spayed, just because is.

What is the most interesting thing you have learned about rabbits?

I have learned that when rabbits arson their hind legs that mean they are happy!

What is your favorite pet rabbit memory? Describe...

My favourite rabbit memory is when I used to have holly, and she used to growl at me and I thought that was because she was making sure the area was safe!

In closing tell us a little about yourself and your bunny...

Well I love my bunnies and I really want to enter them in a local show to get a rosette! And I have recently just got a new baby bunny, he is coming up 8 weeks now, he's black and he is a Netherland Dwarf!

Pet Rabbit Owner Interview #2

Name
Kiersten Carley

Location (City, State/Province, Country)
Stevens Point, WI, USA

About how long have you been a pet rabbit owner?
40 years

What made you want to own a rabbit?
Rabbits are our favorite pets. We enjoy caring for them and showing them at fairs. They seem to enjoy living with us as well.

What is your favorite pet rabbit breed and why?
Our favorites include the English Lop and the French Angora for their looks and personalities.

What advice would you give to a brand new pet rabbit owner?
Be prepared to care for the rabbit about as much as you would care for a dog. Not all rabbits can be outside, all the time depending on the weather.

Do you own more than one pet rabbit? Why or why not?
Yes, currently we have seven rabbits. Sometimes we breed them. We also enjoy having more than one breed with us.

Is your pet rabbit spayed or neutered? Why or why not?
No, because they cannot be altered in order to show them.

What is the most interesting thing you have learned about rabbits?
The joy they bring to my family.

What is your favorite pet rabbit memory? Describe...
The first time I held a rabbit. My dad brought one home for me. I was so happy.

In closing tell us a little about yourself and your bunny...
I have never been without a pet rabbit. I have had many breeds. My children and I continue to keep them as a part of our family. Being without a rabbit is something I cannot imagine.

Pet Rabbit Owner Interview #3

Name
Nic Mason

Location (City, State/Province, Country)
Little Rock, Arkansas

About how long have you been a pet rabbit owner?
6 years

What made you want to own a rabbit?
My family has owned animals for as long as I can remember. We originally had little interest in owning a rabbit but at my school one of the teachers had a rabbit as a class pet and she was retiring and could no longer care for it. The teacher gave us the rabbit and we enjoyed it and since then we have just expanded and are currently still expanding.

What is your favorite pet rabbit breed and why?
My favorite breed is the Dutch rabbits because they are well known for being gentle and calm natured. They are also only about five pounds maximum, so they are not a big rabbit but they are also not a small rabbit.

What advice would you give to a brand new pet rabbit owner?
Avoid exposing the rabbit to direct sunlight. At least make shaded areas available to the rabbit. Also, when cleaning or bathing the rabbit never submerge it in water. The sudden temperature change from the water can cause severe harm to the animal; baby wipes combined with a small position of lemon juice should do the trick very easily. Another thing to watch out for is cedar wood. The smell of cedar shavings has been known to cause respiratory problems for rabbits. Personally I prefer pine shaving.

Do you own more than one pet rabbit? Why or why not?
Yes, I own around many rabbits throughout nine different breeds. I raise rabbits for show and pets.

Is your pet rabbit spayed or neutered? Why or why not?
None of my rabbits are fixed. I am a breeder and raise rabbits.

What is the most interesting thing you have learned about rabbits?

One of the most interesting things I have learned about rabbits is that each rabbit seems to have its own personality, similar to that of a human, and behave accordingly.

What is your favorite pet rabbit memory? Describe...

My favorite rabbit memory is of my rabbit named Chip and myself. He was born here and as he was growing up I played with him and spent time with him every day. Then in May of this year I entered him in the Arkansas State Spring rabbit show and he won 2nd in show. It's one thing for you as an owner to love and enjoy your pet, but it means so much more when someone else such as a judge also sees something special in a pet that already means do much to you.

In closing tell us a little about yourself and your bunny...

My name is Nic and my family and I have a farm. We are members of our local 4H club and raise various types of animals for show as well as pets. It is mainly a hobby of ours and we enjoy doing it together as a family. Our rabbits have been out biggest success as far as showing through the 4H. We treat our rabbits, as well as our other animals, as members of our family.

Pet Rabbit Owner Interview #4

Name
Jessica Mehmel

Location (City, State/Province, Country)
Salem, NJ, USA

About how long have you been a pet rabbit owner?
5 years

What made you want to own a rabbit?
Love their faces and personalities. They make me smile just watching them. They are the love of my life!!!

What is your favorite pet rabbit breed and why?
I love lion heads and holland lops and that's what I raise.

What advice would you give to a brand new pet rabbit owner?
Make sure you go to a breeder not a pet store. They will show you everything you need and help you with any questions you may have. Rabbit breeders have the most knowledge about them. They can tell you things to look for if they are ill and how to treat them...

Do you own more than one pet rabbit? Why or why not?
I have 11 bunnies!!! And each one has their own personality. My bunnies are the best...

Is your pet rabbit spayed or neutered? Why or why not?
No I raise them to sell to 4-hers... I only breed when I'm asked for a specific breed. I don't just breed to breed.

What is the most interesting thing you have learned about rabbits?
I am amazed by how different each and every breed is. No two are alike... they all have different qualities and needs... Care is different for some than others.

What is your favorite pet rabbit memory? Describe...
My favorite memory is the day I got my first lionhead. The excitement I felt was simply over and beyond... He is the love of my life... He will be with me till one day god calls him home.

In closing tell us a little about yourself and your bunny...

I'm 15 years old and I joined 4-h to be able to show my rabbits. I'm proud of all them and have taken many best of breed trophy a home... And each trophy displays their name on it... I am currently going into the 9th grade and still will be raising rabbits. I want to someday be a veterinarian so that I can help all animals as well as rabbits.

Pet Rabbit Owner Interview #5

Name
Aaron Bookman

Location (City, State/Province, Country)
Peyton, CO

About how long have you been a pet rabbit owner?
3 Years

What made you want to own a rabbit?
Selling, looks, behavior.

What is your favorite pet rabbit breed and why?
Holland Lops. Cute, small and very inexpensive to feed.

What advice would you give to a brand new pet rabbit owner?
Contact me for advice. :) My website is: http://bijoubasinrabbitry.com/ .

Do you own more than one pet rabbit? Why or why not?
Yes. Because I do it as a business. Raising and selling adorable Holland lop rabbits.

Is your pet rabbit spayed or neutered? Why or why not?
No, because I breed.

What is the most interesting thing you have learned about rabbits?
They require lots of attention especially in the heat.

What is your favorite pet rabbit memory? Describe...
One of my rabbits was famous. His name was Sharpie. Everybody like him and he liked everybody.

In closing tell us a little about yourself and your bunny...
I own Colorado Springs highest quality Holland Lops and my bunnies are proud of that.

"Bijou Basin Rabbitry now has the top-quality Holland Lops in Colorado Springs. Bred and raised for show. If you are looking for show quality Holland Lops, we have the best one for you."

http://bijoubasinrabbitry.com/

Pet Rabbit Owner Interview #5

Name
Allyson Carl

Location (City, State/Province, Country)
Halifax, PA

About how long have you been a pet rabbit owner?
15 years

What made you want to own a rabbit?
I started showing rabbits in 4-H when I was 8. Rabbits are a great animal for young and old to raise and take care of. They make incredible pets!

What is your favorite pet rabbit breed and why?
I love the French Lops. They have an amazing personality and are like big puppy dogs. Plus, those floppy ears are so gosh darn adorable!

What advice would you give to a brand new pet rabbit owner?
The best advice that I can give is to try new things, and join a club and share your experiences with your beloved pet. 4-H was the best club and I learned so much from people in this organization. Ask questions, and just have fun!

Do you own more than one pet rabbit? Why or why not?
I currently have 20 rabbits (14 adults/6 babies), and three does are bred to have kits in the next couple of weeks. I currently operate Funny Farm Rabbitry, where we breed and raise quality French Lops and Californians.

Is your pet rabbit spayed or neutered? Why or why not?
They are not spayed or neutered. All of my rabbits live in a climate controlled barn.

What is the most interesting thing you have learned about rabbits?
I have learned to have patience and I learned more about the rabbit industry and unusual breeds.

What is your favorite pet rabbit memory? Describe...

My favorite memory is when I won best of show at my local fair with a French Lop that I raised from a kit.

In closing tell us a little about yourself and your bunny...

The picture That I included is of one of my French Lop juniors. This was one out 6 in the litter and is special to me because this was the first little of French Lops that I raised while starting out Funny Farm Rabbitry as a business. The second picture is of one of my Californian does and I while I was the reigning Fair Queen. I was giving a presentation on rabbits at a local elementary school.

http://funnyfarmrabbitryfrenchlops.weebly.com/

http://funnyfarmrabbitryfrenchlops.weebly.com/

Pet Rabbit Owner Interview #6

Name
Monica Rohatynchuk

Location (City, State/Province, Country)
McBride, BC, Canada

About how long have you been a pet rabbit owner?
25 years

What made you want to own a rabbit?
Rabbits have a wonderful thing about them that I am attracted to. Most people look at these creatures as useless rodents. They are very smart as well as cute and cuddly. I have litter trained mine, house trained them, they are very social and playful, great with kids and other animals.

What is your favorite pet rabbit breed and why?
I love the Flemish Giants. Just more of them to love!

What advice would you give to a brand new pet rabbit owner?
Make sure you do your home work and understand they are a forever pet and not a spur of the moment decision because they are cute. Understand to pros and cons to being a rabbit owner. Research they climate you live in and how your new pet will adapt. Understand they do need to be groomed, nails trimmed, and they need to chew due to their teeth are always growing.

Do you own more than one pet rabbit? Why or why not?
Yes, for many reasons. We have several of our own pets and we also rescue rabbits from others who can no longer provide the proper care they need.

Is your pet rabbit spayed or neutered? Why or why not?
Yes, we have several of our furry friends spayed and neutered so they do not multiply and we do have a does and bucks who are not because we breed them once maybe twice a year.

What is the most interesting thing you have learned about rabbits?
You can teach them tricks and they can learn their names

What is your favorite pet rabbit memory? Describe...

Having a Holland Lop who played in our yard with our children and would not be leashed. She was out on her own just like a cat or dog and she would chase birds.

In closing tell us a little about yourself and your bunny...

I am a mother of 3. I had my first pet rabbit at the age of three. I have loved the creatures ever since. I have bred and raised for show and pets from the age of 12. In the past 7 years I have started rescuing rabbits from rabbit mills, from families who can no longer provide a home or want to provide homes for their rabbits, and from the local SPCA's when their facilities start to get too full. We spay and neuter our rabbits who are not used for breeding. We have converted the back of our barn in to a rabbit wonderland. We have pens with play equipment, blocks, tunnels, and outdoor runs plus out friend come into our home and enjoy playing with our kids, cat and Saint Bernard dogs. We enjoy our Flemish Giants cuddling with us on our couch! They put a smile on our faces each and every day.

Pet Rabbit Owner Interview #7

Name
Alyssa Stucky

Location (City, State/Province, Country)
Newton, Kansas, USA

About how long have you been a pet rabbit owner?
About 5 Years

What made you want to own a rabbit?
They seemed like easy and fun pets and I was interested in showing them at the county fair.

What is your favorite pet rabbit breed and why?
My favorite breed is the Mini Rex, they have amazing fur and are super friendly pets. There are so many different color variations that its always a surprise when you have a new litter. They show really well and don't require too much maintenance.

What advice would you give to a brand new pet rabbit owner?
Invest time into showing your rabbit at fairs, even though it takes extra time and work, you will learn a lot about the structure of your animal and meet other breeders.

Do you own more than one pet rabbit? Why or why not?
Yes, I show and breed to sell. When I show I like to have the best selection to choose from.

Is your pet rabbit spayed or neutered? Why or why not?
No, I breed and sell my rabbits to other wanting to breed them.

What is the most interesting thing you have learned about rabbits?
When they get excited they will jump up in the air a kick out their back legs, its a lot of fun to watch.

What is your favorite pet rabbit memory? Describe...
One of the rabbits from my litter, a couple months after it looked like it had a seizure. Its head was tilted and it ran around in circles. We put it in another pen with another rabbit and raised the water and feeder so that it would have to try to raise its head to get food. A couple weeks

later it was completely back to normal, hopping in straight lines and its head was held straight. we are now preparing to get that rabbit ready for show time and its one of the best in the pens.

In closing tell us a little about yourself and your bunny...
We have a lot of fun learning tricks, playing outside, and winning ribbons. Having a rabbit is a lot of fun and not too much work.

Pet Rabbit Owner Interview #8

Name
Kenneth Newby

Location (City, State/Province, Country)
Hamlet, NC

About how long have you been a pet rabbit owner?
6 months

What made you want to own a rabbit?
I love the Flemish and wanted some.

What is your favorite pet rabbit breed and why?
Flemish - The size and they are real docile.

What advice would you give to a brand new pet rabbit owner?
Learn about the breed you want. Get everything in place and build or buy the proper housing so you do not have to upgrade as the rabbit grows.

Do you own more than one pet rabbit? Why or why not?
No, I like the different colors of the breed.

Is your pet rabbit spayed or neutered? Why or why not?
No, These are rare rabbits and I want to help keep them established.

What is the most interesting thing you have learned about rabbits?
The feeding of babies and how the mom takes care of them is just awesome.

What is your favorite pet rabbit memory? Describe...
My first rabbit and how it just took to me!

In closing tell us a little about yourself and your bunny...
We have several Flemish rabbits. I work at home and so I can take care of them. If I just fed and left, could take me 20 minutes. But I don't. Everyone needs attention. So, My feeding regiment takes a while!

Pet Rabbit Owner Interview #9

Name
Jenny Fox

Location (City, State/Province, Country)
Troy, WV, USA

About how long have you been a pet rabbit owner?
3 years

What made you want to own a rabbit?
I had bunnies as a child and was very fond of them and wanted to have some as an adult and share the experience with my children. We all love them and spoil them as we do all our other pets.

What is your favorite pet rabbit breed and why?
Holland lops because they seem to my experience to be one of the most mild and friendly breeds, usually loving and easy going. They are small in size and easy to handle and I love the lop ears.

What advice would you give to a brand new pet rabbit owner?
Make sure you are ready for a new bunny before you get it. Research and learn all you can about them first because bunnies are a commitment and have many needs. They are very unique animals but also very smart and can even be litter trained. Be prepared to give them lots of attention and time.

Do you own more than one pet rabbit? Why or why not?
Yes because I love having them around seeing each one with its own personality. I have a small little rabbitry where each bunny has its own special place and is treated like family and very spoiled.

Is your pet rabbit spayed or neutered? Why or why not?
None are at this time but I plan on doing this in the future with some

What is the most interesting thing you have learned about rabbits?
They are so smart and can be litter trained and I just love watching them do binkies!

What is your favorite pet rabbit memory? Describe...

I have so many it is hard to narrow it down to one. I guess the one I think of first is when my angora doe, Ellie had her first babies. She had them early, not in the nest box and some had crawled out of the cage and were cold when I found them, 8 in all. She was frantic and scared. I scooped them all up and put them on a heating pad and blanket and got their little bodies warmed up. Soon they were wiggling around. She hadn't prepared for them yet. I think she was just unsure about what to do this being her first litter. So I held her on my lap and pulled her hair out on her belly for her and used it in her nest box. Then I held each baby to her one by and they ate. She was so patient and just set on my lap through it all. We bonded and it was such a wonderful experience. I have a special place in my heart for my Ellie girl. We only lost one baby that morning and the rest grew into very pretty bunnies. I still have two of them.

In closing tell us a little about yourself and your bunny...

I am married and a mother of 4. We are all pet lovers and have several kinds of pets. we have several bunnies also and each one has its own name and unique personality. We just started out with a couple but loved the experience with raising babies so much we decided to raise them regularly. We find them good loving homes and get so much joy out of doing this. My kids have learned so much about caring for little animals from them. We spoil them and give them lots of love. We bring them in and let them play and take them for walks. My Holland lop bunny, marshmallow is an indoor bunny who practically rules the house! She has a silly personality and loves to eat her goodies!

Pet Rabbit Owner Interview #10

Name
Traci Thysell-McPherson

Location (City, State/Province, Country)
Silverton, OR, USA

About how long have you been a pet rabbit owner?
2 years this time around.

What made you want to own a rabbit?
Have always loved rabbits, have a deep love of animals and it seemed to be God ordained. I rescued my Giant American Chinchilla rabbit, Princess Jewel from eventually being slaughtered. She is now a pet therapy bun. :) And a 3 time 1st place winner in costume contests and pet parades.

What is your favorite pet rabbit breed and why?
I think they are all lovely, but I have to say I have a partiality to Giant Chinchilla and Angora breeds. I like the coloring of the chins as well as their character and the wooliness of Angoras.

What advice would you give to a brand new pet rabbit owner?
Study up on how to be a good owner, make sure that a rabbits personality and needs will fit into your life style before getting one, study their habits, what training it will take, what foods are best and what are no, no's. Search out rabbit associations in your area and find a good exotic pet veterinarian.

Do you own more than one pet rabbit? Why or why not?
Just one at present, but would like to find a mate to bond with my lil' princess.

Is your pet rabbit spayed or neutered? Why or why not?
Not spayed at present. While I know it is important health wise and responsibility wise I would like to breed my rabbit once, but still deciding on this.

What is the most interesting thing you have learned about rabbits?
Jewelie teaches me things almost daily, but I suppose that when you understand the nature of a rabbit, the best ways to approach them and that they are very social and loving animals . . . they can become great family members.

What is your favorite pet rabbit memory? Describe...
The joy she brings to not only me daily, but everyone she comes in contact with.

In closing tell us a little about yourself and your bunny...
Princess Jewel is a bundle of love and fluff. She is at last weigh in 16.5 lbs, 28 inches long and believe it or not the runt of the litter. She was rescued by love. PJ lives with 2 male cats, both rescues in their own right, Mercy a gray tortise shell tabby & Love a pixiebob whom she is dominant over. She is otherwise very docile. Of course loves attention, is litter box trained and while not recommended for most rabbits she loves to be held like a baby. Not knowing, she has been held this way since she was 5 weeks old. Jewelie was fed goats milk with a syringe as she was yet still to young to be weaned from her momma. She is full of sweetness!

Pet Rabbit Owner Interview #11

Name
Crystal Milbauer

Location (City, State/Province, Country)
Grafton

About how long have you been a pet rabbit owner?
1 and 1/2 years

What made you want to own a rabbit?
I always wanted to own rabbits ever since I was little.

What is your favorite pet rabbit breed and why?
Mini Lops due to their personality and size.

What advice would you give to a brand new pet rabbit owner?
Every rabbit is different. You need to find the right on. Be patient with your new bun. When getting a new bun let him settle in his/her cage for a few days and they start talking to the bun and petting him/her. You want to build a bond between the 2 of you. Spend time getting him/her out of the cage to play it can be very rewarding. If you are worried about the bun going to the bathroom on the floor there is a easy fix. Litter box train, it is very easy. Find the spot in the cage where your bun is going. Scoop out the dirty area and place it in a Litter box pan with clean shavings. Place the box in the cage and one on the floor where the bun plays. You can show the bun where the box is and he/she should use it. Buns are so fun to have as a pet and always do research before getting any pet. You can find get buns anywhere. Buns love to give kisses, pet, some like to be held, even go for wagon or car rides. Mine do! Having a bun is so rewarding!! Enjoy!

Do you own more than one pet rabbit? Why or why not?
Yes. I feel like some buns like to have a playmate to keep the company. Some of mine are with other buns and some are not.

Is your pet rabbit spayed or neutered? Why or why not?
No, I don't have any spayed because I have a very small rabbitry and I do breed my buns from time to time. I love raising the kit and finding great pet homes and seeing the customers faces

when they pick up there little ones. If you are looking for just a pet bun then I recommend spaying if you don't want to breed. :)

What is the most interesting thing you have learned about rabbits?
Their personalities! I have mini lops that love to give kisses, run circles around you, love attention. I also have a English Lop that acts like a dog. She has her own spot on the couch. I never thought buns acted like this. I love it!!!
What is your favorite pet rabbit memory? Describe...
My first bun I ever got when I was a kid. His name was Moe. Broken Black Mini Lop.

In closing tell us a little about yourself and your bunny...
Well I live in the country and have 9 buns. They are my babies. I put their health and well being 1st! All my buns have a forever home with me. My buns get time out of their cages to play around the house. They are kept inside, I feel like that is a safe spot for them and I can always watch them.

The photo is me with my English lop willow. She is so like a dog in many ways. I love her so much!

Pet Rabbit Owner Interview #12

Name
Bailey Hiersche

Location (City, State/Province, Country)
Lawrence, KS

About how long have you been a pet rabbit owner?
5+ years

What made you want to own a rabbit?
My friend was in 4H, and she had rabbits, and I have always have been an animal lover, only allowed to have hermit crabs until I FINALLY convinced my parents to let me have a rabbit (: and I have had them ever since

What is your favorite pet rabbit breed and why?
Can't pick, I like English Angoras, French Angoras, and Jersey Woolys, also Mini lops, in which were my very first rabbits breed.

What advice would you give to a brand new pet rabbit owner?
Make sure you are ready for a commitment

Do you own more than one pet rabbit? Why or why not?
Yes! Because I love them!!

Is your pet rabbit spayed or neutered? Why or why not?
No, I show them in 4H, in 4H they cannot be spayed/neutered to be shown.

What is the most interesting thing you have learned about rabbits?
They all have such different personalities; although in the different breeds you see that their personalities really vary throughout the breeds also, not just throughout the rabbits.

What is your favorite pet rabbit memory? Describe...
My very first rabbit, Ginger, I remember him all the time! he was just like my little pet dog (: he would follow me around everywhere, all the time!!

In closing tell us a little about yourself and your bunny...

I am a Teenager in Kansas, I just love animals, and I will be a large animal vet when I grow up, I have several Angora rabbits I show, and use their angora for fiber arts!

http://hersheycreekrabbits.weebly.com/
https://www.facebook.com/HersheyCreekRabbits

Pet Rabbit Owner Interview #13

Name
Julie Brinton

Location (City, State/Province, Country)
Bolivar

About how long have you been a pet rabbit owner?
6 months

What made you want to own a rabbit?
Originally got them for commercial purposes but one stole our hearts!

What is your favorite pet rabbit breed and why?
Californian, love the markings.

What advice would you give to a brand new pet rabbit owner?
Give them plenty of attention.

Do you own more than one pet rabbit? Why or why not?
Yes, we have 9 all together. Raising some for commercial purposes, also the droppings are great in the garden.

Is your pet rabbit spayed or neutered? Why or why not?
No, don't see a need to.

What is the most interesting thing you have learned about rabbits?
They each have their own personalities.

What is your favorite pet rabbit memory? Describe...
None, yet but will hopefully make some soon.

In closing tell us a little about yourself and your bunny...
Our bunny only has one ear. She was born this way. She is full of spunk even though she isn't like the other rabbits. She is our little Nemo!

Pet Rabbit Owner Interview #14

Name
Melissa Morey

Location (City, State/Province, Country)
Ireland

About how long have you been a pet rabbit owner?
The day I was born my family owned rabbits.

What made you want to own a rabbit?
My family had always reared and raised rabbits! I just loved their big personalities. I saw videos on YouTube of people showing their rabbits and it just made me want to buy a rabbit!

What is your favorite pet rabbit breed and why?
My personal favorite pet rabbit breed is the Holland Lop Rabbit. I love these rabbits because they have a huge personality in my experience. They make great pets. Also in my experience with them they get on great with other family pets (i.e dogs, guinea pigs and other rabbits). The Holland lop is a great rabbit, not too big so it's easy to handle and house them. I just love the Holland lops!

What advice would you give to a brand new pet rabbit owner?
I would say if your brand new research is a great thing. I know YouTube videos helped me ALOT! Especially when it comes to food, you may need help so research is definitely key. I'd also say enjoy your experience. Rabbits are loveable animals and you should definitely make the most of the time you have with them.

Do you own more than one pet rabbit? Why or why not?
Yes, i have always owned more than one rabbit. I do this because i fear they'd become lonely without a companion. At the moment I have four French lop rabbits.
I think rabbits are sociable and in my opinion love other rabbits.

Is your pet rabbit spayed or neutered? Why or why not?
No at the moment my rabbits aren't spayed/neutered because i wanted to breed them.

What is the most interesting thing you have learned about rabbits?

The most interesting thing i have learned about rabbits is their intelligence! Rabbits can be taught commands and tricks! I think it's mind-blowing!

What is your favorite pet rabbit memory? Describe...
My favourite memory is discovering my rabbit was after having babies! The babies were born in a burrow. One morning I looked out my window to see little fur balls playing in the run! I think i cried with joy!

In closing tell us a little about yourself and your bunny...
This is Levi! Our female Lionhead, bred from one of our other rabbits. Levi is the most playful bunny you could meet. She loves to follow me around the pen and enjoys nibbling on carrots!

Pet Rabbit Owner Interview #15

Name
Laura Rabinson

Location (City, State/Province, Country)
Bendigo, Victoria, Australia

About how long have you been a pet rabbit owner?
I have raised rabbits for over 5 years.

What made you want to own a rabbit?
I love animals to start with and getting my fist purebred rabbit (Dwarf Lop) was exiting. When I was younger my parents had always allowed us to keep rabbits as pets and me and my brother really enjoyed them. Soon after I purchased my dwarf lop buck, I asked if I could get a female as well, to breed with. And so now I have ended up with a small breeding program, made up of 3 pure bred does and a buck.

What is your favorite pet rabbit breed and why?
I love Dwarf Lops. It is mostly because of their lovely temperament. Nearly all dwarf lops I have owned, have been very laid back, relaxed rabbits that like human interaction. I also like the shape of dwarf lop rabbits. I think their round boofy heads are so cute, and they are fairly small so they are also easy to handle. There is a range of colors also available in dwarf lops, so there lots to choose from too!

What advice would you give to a brand new pet rabbit owner?
Give it some thought before you actually buy a rabbit. Make sure you can provide it with a cage, food, water, attention and proper care. New rabbit owners should read up on how to look after rabbits. I would recommend visiting http://www.therabbitpatch.com.au/

Do you own more than one pet rabbit? Why or why not?
I currently have 4 rabbits. I would love to get more for my breeding program but I wouldn't have to time with my schooling and busy lifestyle. I hope to one day have some extra time so I am able to raise more rabbits.

Is your pet rabbit spayed or neutered? Why or why not?
None of my rabbits are de-sexed, they are apart of my breeding program.

What is the most interesting thing you have learned about rabbits?
There is nothing I find terribly interesting about rabbits. I just enjoy them for their own little personalities and characteristics.

What is your favorite pet rabbit memory? Describe...
My favorite memory was when I had my first successful litter of bunnies. I was so excited to raise them up to the sage at which I could find them new homes.

In closing tell us a little about yourself and your bunny...
I have a close connection to my bunnies and my rabbits know me, a lot more than the other people in my family. They love to be handled by myself but when they are being handled by someone else they tend to become a bit nervous. My bunnies are always happy to see me when I go outside and the bounce up and down their cage, wanting some attention. This is very cute!

101 Pet Rabbit Name Ideas

Alfalfa	Daisy	Napoleon
Alfie	Dancer	Noah
Angel	Dandelion	Oliver
Angora	Diamond	Oreo
Annabelle	Domino	Peanut
Autumn	Dutchess	Pebbles
Baby	Elfie	Pepper
Bambi	Elvis	Petter
Barbi	Enegizer Bunny	Petter Cottontail
Basil	Eve	Poppy
Bella	Floppy	Princess
Binky	Flopsy	Pumpkin
Bluebell	Frosty	Queen
Bugs	Ginger	Ralph
Bun Bun	Goofy	Rasberry
Bunnicula	Happy	Rascal
Bunzilla	Harry	Romeo
Caesar	Hazel	Smokey
Carrot	Hershey	Sniffles
Cecil	Honey	Snowflake
Charlie	Isabelle	Sweetie
Ceckers	Jack	Thumper
Chief	James	Thunder
Chloe	James Bond	Twinkles
Chocolate	Jessie	Vanilla
Chuck	John	Velvet
Cocoa	King	Velveteen
Coffee	Kitten	Whiskers
Cookie	Lady	Whisper
Copper	Lucy	Willow
Cosmo	Marshmallow	Yosemite
Crystal	Misty	Zeus
Cupid	Mustang	Zoe
Cutiepie	Nancy	

Chapter 5: Rabbit Resources/Glossary and Final Words

Resources for Rabbit Owners

Here is a listing of rabbit resources that I recommend that every rabbit owner at least check out for various reasons. By taking advantage of the resources mentioned within this section of the book you can learn more about raising rabbits and potentially save money on your pet rabbit supplies.

Resource #1: PremiumRabbits.com

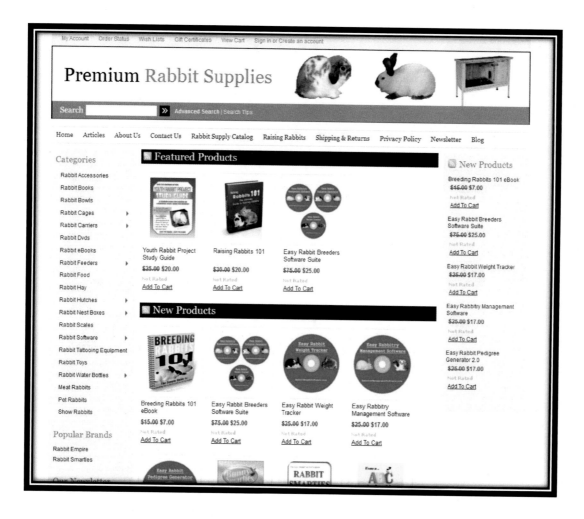

Description: If you are in search of pet rabbit supplies, PremiumRabbits.com is the website that you need to check out. PremiumRabbits.com "provides you will top quality rabbit supplies at affordable prices". Using the site you can find pet rabbit cages, carriers, food, feeders and MUCH more!

URL: http://premiumrabbits.com/

Resource #2: Raising Rabbits 101 Book

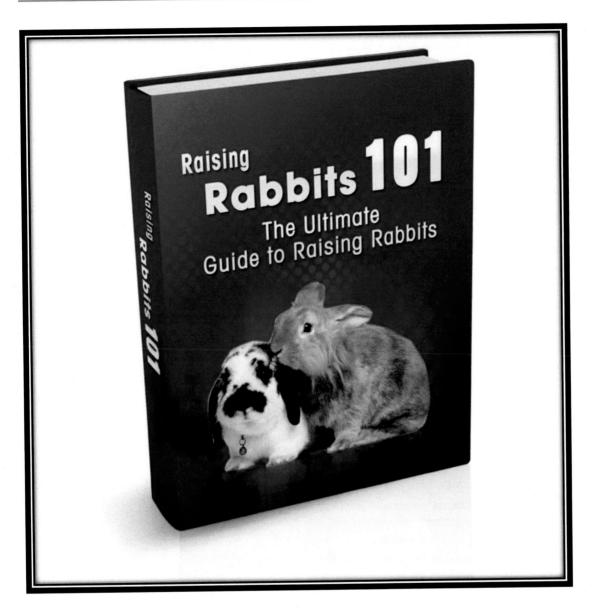

Description: If you are interested in learning more about raising rabbits or want to start breeding your own, Raising Rabbits 101 is the book for you. Raising Rabbits 101 contains information on a huge range of subjects ranging from kindling to feeding to breeding to marketing and Much, Much more. This book has labeled by some as being the "Ultimate Guide to Raising Rabbits". The book is available in both soft cover and eBook format. Grab yourself a copy today...

URL: http://raisingrabbits101.com/

Resource #3: RabbitBreeders.us (This one is FREE)

Description: At RabbitBreeders.us you can access the World's Largest Rabbit Breeders Directory, in which I am proud to say that I assembled myself, with the intent of providing a great free resource for helping rabbit enthusiasts like yourself find rabbits for sale. Since establishing the website, RabbitBreeders.us has received over 1.4 million visits from rabbit raisers all around the World! I also have taken the time to establish two sister sites, one for Canada and the other for England that can be accessed via RabbitBreeders.ca and RabbitBreeders.org.uk. This is a terrific free resource that you can't afford not to check out if you are looking to find pet rabbits for sale :)

URL: http://rabbitbreeders.us/

Resource #4: The Youth Rabbit Project Study Guide

Description: If you are interested in showing a rabbit I suggest that you grab yourself a copy of a really cool rabbit book titled: The Youth Rabbit Project Study Guide. Within this guide you will learn all about things such as rabbit showmanship, rabbit show preparation and other topics of that nature, which will help you get started in the rabbit showing industry.

URL: http://www.premiumrabbits.com/youth-rabbit-project-study-guide/

Resource #5: The Easy Rabbit Pedigree Generator

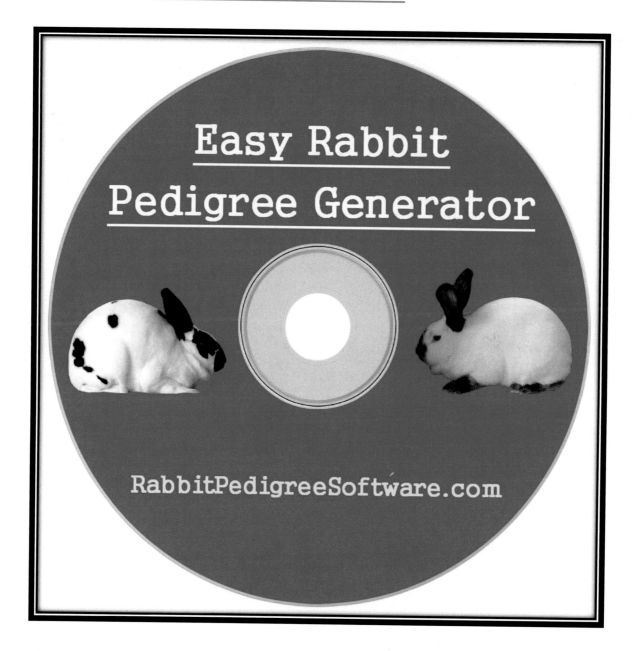

Description: If you are ever interested in creating pedigrees for your rabbits, I suggest that you grab yourself a copy of The Easy Rabbit Pedigree Generator. This piece of software is much lower in price than any of the other solutions on the market and is very simple to use. There is almost zero learning curve to the program, meaning that you can start creating your own pedigrees within minutes after installation.

URL: http://rabbitpedigreesoftware.com/

Resource #6: TheRabbitMentor.com

Description: If you are interested in becoming a rabbit breeder and raising your own rabbits, this is the resource for you. The Rabbit Mentor is essentially a membership website that was built with the sole purpose of training rabbit raisers on the various aspects of their project. As a member of The Rabbit Mentor Program you will receive monthly raising rabbits training videos that will vary in topic ranging from breeding to feeding to housing to marketing and MUCH more. If you are interested in becoming a member, you will be happy to learn that we are currently offering a HUGE discount on the program. Check it out today!

URL: http://therabbitmentor.com/

Resource #7: AMAZON.COM

Description: Amazon is a great place to find many different pet rabbit supplies for sale. This is a particularly good place to shop if you live outside the United States and are having a hard time trying to find a company that will ship. On Amazon you can find my first book Raising Rabbits 101 in addition to other products we have produced.

URL: http://rabbitbreeders.us/amazon

Final Words:

Dear Friend,

Owning and caring for a pet rabbit can be a truly exciting experience, that you are bound to enjoy.

I recommend that you spend an adequate amount of time selecting yourself a desired rabbit breed before getting started, as there are so many great possibilities!

If you are indeed serious about successfully caring for your pet rabbit I also recommend before getting your rabbit that you read through this entire book and check out the recommend resources. In particular it is recommended that you visit **http://premiumrabbits.com/** to order your pet rabbit supplies, and then visit **http://rabbitbreeders.us/** to locate a rabbit breeder in your area.

 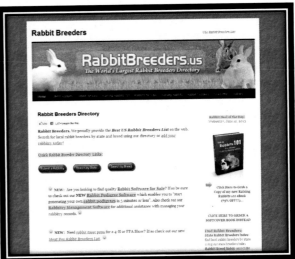

I also have included various links to resources within this book that will aid you if you would like to ever get involved in raising or showing rabbits yourself.

In closing let me just say that I wish you the best of luck and happiness in your pet rabbit adventure!

Happy Rabbit Owning + Take Care,

Sincerely,

Your Friend

Aaron "The Rabbit Master" Webster

Abbreviated Glossary for Pet Rabbit Raisers

List of terms and abbreviations pertaining to pet rabbit owners- next page contains definitions

Abscess

Adult

ARBA

Back

Bare Spot

Belly

Bloodline

Breeder

Buck

Buck-Teeth

Cheek

Chest

Chopped

Class

Classification

Convention

Crossbred

Dewlap

Doe

Domestic Rabbit

DQ

Ear Canker

Feces

Fertility

Foot

Forehead

Fostering

Gestation

Hip

Hock

Inner Ear

Inventory

Kindling

Kit

Knee

Litter

Malocclusion

Molting

Nest box

Pair

Palpation

Parasite

Pathogen

Pedigree

Rabbit Cage

Rabbit Hutch

Rabbitry

Registration

Snuffles

Tattoo

Trio

Weaning

Wolf Teeth

Youth Exhibitor

Abbreviated Rabbit Terms and Definitions

A

Abscess- a lump on a rabbit's skin which is hard and filled with pus

Adult- in most rabbit breed shows which have four main breed classes, an adult rabbit is considered to be a rabbit that is at least six months of age or older

ARBA- acronym for the American Rabbit Breeders Association

B

Back- the portion of a rabbit which extends from the neck to the tail

Bare Spot- any portion on a rabbit's body that lacks fur due to a molt, fur mites or another cause

Belly- the lower section of a rabbit's body which contains the abdomen and intestines

Bloodline- a term used to describe the ancestry of a given rabbit or herd; usually in terms of physical and genetic makeup (Example: This rabbit came from Joe Jone's winning bloodline!)

Breeder- a term used to describe any rabbit raiser which produces offspring with his or her herd, or a rabbit which is used to breed

Buck- a common name used to refer to a male rabbit

Buck-Teeth- a trait that is usually genetic, which refers to a form of malocclusion in which a rabbit's teeth meet together evenly instead of the upper teeth overlapping the bottom teeth

C

Cheek- the portion of a rabbit's face below its eyes

Chest- the front portion of a rabbit's body between its forelegs and neck

Chopped- a rabbit which lacks overall balance; usually refers to a rabbit lacking in the upper or lower hindquarters

Class- a group of rabbits that fall into the same gender, pattern and age group

Classification- a system of arranging or identifying rabbits

Convention- the national or state based rabbit show which is held by ARBA

Crossbred- a rabbit which has direct ancestors from more than one rabbit breed

D

Dewlap- the flap of extra fat under a rabbit's chin; usually only seen on does

Doe- a common name used to refer to a female rabbit

Domestic Rabbit- a rabbit that has been bred to specifically live in human captivity

DQ- any show rabbit disqualification, trait many times caused by weak genetics

E

Ear Canker- an inflamed scabby condition inside a rabbit's ear caused by an infestation of the ear canal by ear mites; especially common in warm and moist southern climates

F

Feces- rabbit waste products, manure

Fertility- term refers to a rabbit's ability to "get bred" or simply to reproduce

Foot- the part of the leg on which a rabbit stands

Forehead- the section of a rabbit's head between the eyes and base of the ears

Fostering- the process of taking kits from the mother rabbit, and placing them in the nest box of another doe; many breeders have different opinions about this technique

G

Gestation- the period of time between breeding and kindling

H

Hip- the thigh joint and large first joint of a rabbit's hind leg

Hock- the middle joint or section of a rabbit's hind leg which is located between the foot and hip

I

Inner Ear- the inwardly curved, concave portion of a rabbit's ear

Inventory- list of all supplies and rabbits that you currently own

K

Kindling- the process of giving birth to young offspring

Kit- the proper term for a baby rabbit

Knee- the second joint of the leg which connects the thigh and leg together

L

Litter- a mother's offspring, group of bunnies

M

Malocclusion- the misalignment of a rabbit's teeth

Molting- the process in which a rabbit sheds an existing layer of fur; in warm climates a rabbit usually "molts" during the summer months

N

Nest Box- a box provided to a doe so that she can prepare a nest for her soon to be arriving bunnies inside of it, also called kindling box or simply "bunny box"

P

Pair- a term that usually refers to a couple of rabbits consisting of a male and a female

Palpation- the process of feeling a doe's abdomen with the hopes of determining whether or not the doe is pregnant

Parasite- an organism that is harmful to the well being of your rabbits

Pathogen- any living organism that causes disease

Pedigree- a record keeping paper which shows the ancestry of a given rabbit, normally between 3 and 5 generations are shown

R

Rabbit Cage- an enclosed structure where rabbits are contained; normally made of wire, sometimes wood

Rabbit Hutch- any enclosed structure in which rabbit are kept; usually made of wood, wire or both

Rabbitry- any place where domestic rabbits are raised or kept

Registration- the process of getting a rabbit registered by an organization such as ARBA

S

Snuffles- a contagious nasal or lung infection that rabbits can "catch"

T

Tattoo- an identification mechanism used to indentify rabbits by the process of placing a letter or number marking in one of their two ears

Trio- generally a "trio" of rabbits consists of three breeding age rabbits; 2 does and a buck

W

Weaning- a term used to describe the process during which bunnies begin to grow independent of their mother for nourishment; Some breeders will forcibly wean kits between 4 and 8 weeks of age, others leave the bunnies with their mothers for a longer period of time

Wolf Teeth- protruding teeth in a rabbit's upper and lower jaw which is caused by the improper alignment of the upper and lower front teeth, preventing them from being grinded down naturally; generally breeders will automatically cull all rabbits with wolf teeth

Y

Youth Exhibitor- exhibitors under age 19

Made in the USA
Columbia, SC
25 June 2023